Santiago Gonzalez

Assisted by

María José Quevedo
Leonor Bravo
Verónica Tapia
Luis Apunte
Sanqui Boada

First published in 2011 by Ediciones independientes

Book design by Santiago González
The main text was set in Thors Thunderfont

www.edicionesindependientes.com

Av. El Inca E4-340 e Isla Seymour,
(593) 92583596
Quito, Ecuador

ISBN- 978-9942-03-946

Printed in Ecuador by Ediecuatorial

EDIEC 11647

THE ONLY ONE

Ei!
Ediciones independientes

SANTIAGO GONZÁLEZ

Here, the land is small,
the sea is big
and the sky is bigger.

N
NE
E
SE
S
SW
W
NW

A long time ago,
a voyager arrived
to this small universe,

and more came slowly,
one after another.

From sea, land, and air,

all together formed a new tribe.

The differences didn't matter,

either with fins,

wings

legs

feathers

scales

beaks

or snouts
with teeth,

each one found
its own place.

While taking a
break on dry land or
among branches,

While taking flight
towards the horizon,

or submerging into the sea.

All of them adapted
to the new environment;
some with subtle variations.
All sources of inspiration
for a good spectator.
9
8
12
2

10
7
4
13
11
1
5
3
6

Now you can observe them,
grouped in a flock

shoal

or herd.

Or in perfect balance
wherever they go,

as good fellow travelers
and neighbors.

Through the day,
wherever you look,
you can find creatures
of all sizes and shapes,

in small or large
numbers.

Except for
one,
because this one is
unique.
He is the only one.

He was born from an egg
many years ago,

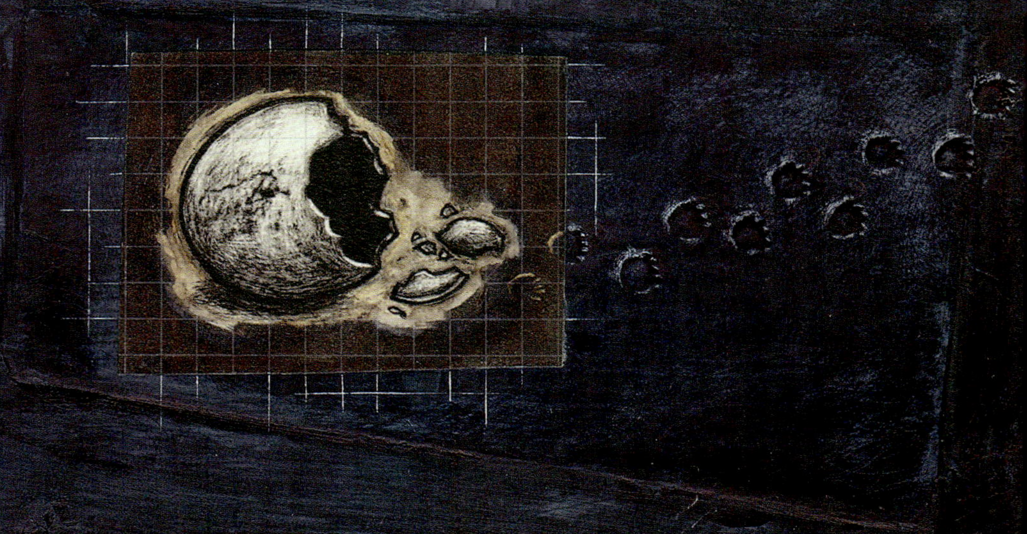

and he grew up to be a giant
like his ancestors.

The giant
has a nickname,
LONESOME,
and a single name,
GEORGE.

But George was not so lonely.

In the past, he was part of a unique and primitive family.

Nowadays
George is the last member
of that family.

However, he stands
for all endangered species.

VISUAL GLOSSARY

LONESOME GEORGE

He is the last known individual of the Pinta Island giant tortoise. This small island is located in the North of the Galapagos Archipelago, and it was once home to thousands of tortoises. Whalers and sealers heavily depleted the numbers of these giants in the 19th century. The tortoises were a good food source as they could live up to a year in the holds of the ships without food and water.

George was first seen on the island of Pinta on 1971. It was decided to bring the animal back to the Charles Darwin Research Station, where they have made every effort to encourage him to breed with female tortoises of a different subspecies, the closest morphologically to the Pinta tortoises. Yet over the past years of trying, no new tortoises have been born.

George has been labeled the rarest creature in the world, and he is a potent symbol for conservation efforts in the Galapagos Islands and conservation efforts internationally. George is estimated to be between 60 and 90 years old, and he is in good health.

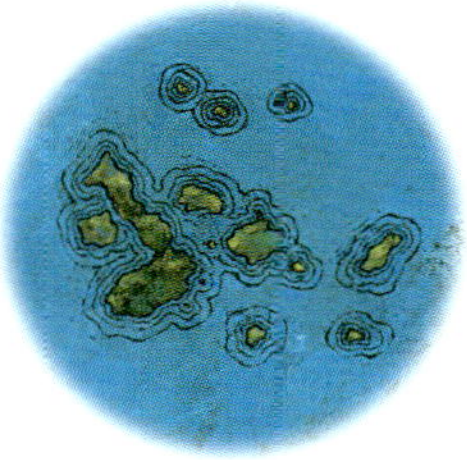

THE GALAPAGOS ISLANDS

It is an archipelago of volcanic islands distributed around the equator in the Pacific Ocean, 972 Km. west of continental Ecuador, of which they are a part. The group consists of 13 main islands, 6 smaller islands, and 107 rocks and islets. These islands had a volcanic origin separate from the mainlaind and were never connected to it. This way, the oldest islands would have originated about 5 millions ago of, while the newest would only be 700.000 years old.

Anyone of the species here present, in some moment had to cross more than 1.000 Km. of ocean and theoretically this could only have been made in three ways: floating in the sea or in a natural raft; dispersed by the wind or flying; or transported in the body of another organism, for air or for sea.

H.M.S. BEAGLE

It was originally a ship of war of the Royal Navy, but did not ever participate in a battle. She was then adapted as a survey barque and took part in three expeditions. On the second survey voyage, which set sail from England on December 1831, the young naturalist Charles Darwin was on board, and his work would eventually make the Beagle one of the most famous ships in history.

GALAPAGOS LAND IGUANA

It is endemic to the Galapagos Islands. The Galapagos land iguana varies in morphology and coloration among different island populations. They have a life expectancy of up to 60 years.

FLIGHTLESS CORMORANT

The flightless cormorant evolved in an isolated island environment, that was free of land predators. As a result, the birds had no need to fly and eventually the species became flightless.

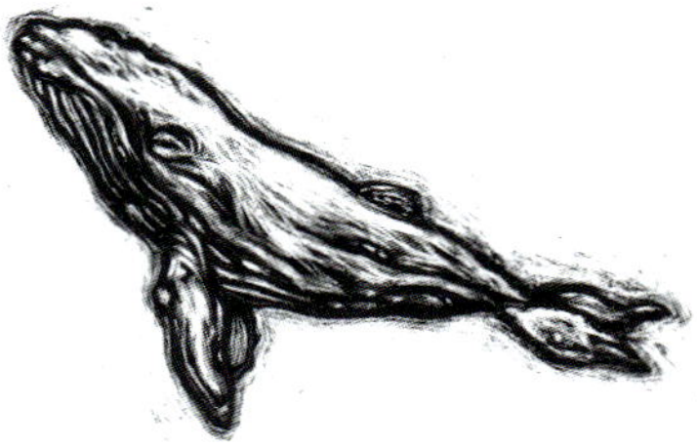

HUMPBACK WHALE

It is an amazing marine colossus. These humpback whales migrate all the way down from the Antarctic regions in an attempt to find a mating partner in order to reproduce.

GALAPAGOS PENGUIN

It is a penguin endemic to the Galapagos Islands. The strong sun is the main problem for the penguins. During the cool nights they sleep and nest on the land.

GALAPAGOS HAWK

This is one of the predators of the finches and other birds on the Galapagos Islands. The hawks also prey on insects, rats, and small lizards.

NAZCA BOOBY

Adult birds are easily identified with their beautiful white head, gray legs and feet, body and wing coverts, dark tails, masks, and patches on their backs.

RAZOR SURGEONFISH

Generally grey with bright yellow tail fin; a few black spots on tail base; a dark bar through eye and another through shoulder. Maximum size, about 60 cm.

BROWN PELICAN

These pelicans can be seen especially around the harbors of most islands in Galapagos. They lay their eggs usually between two or three and they both (male and female) share incubation for about four weeks.

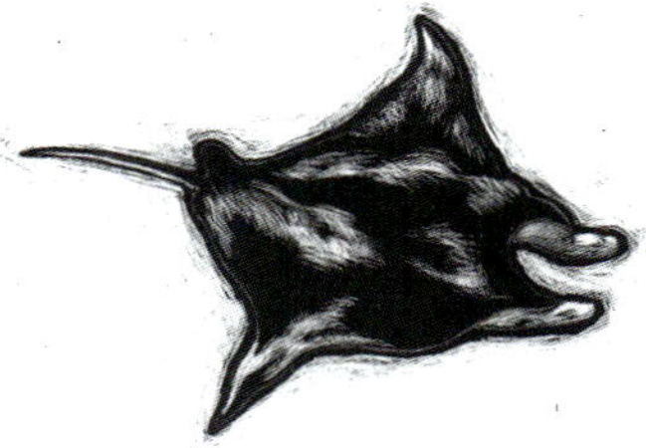

MANTA RAY OR GIANT MANTA

It is the largest of the rays. Manta rays have a diamond shaped body which helps then swim gracefully through the water using their pectoral fins as 'wings'. They have the biggest brains of any fish.

GALAPAGOS PARROTFISH

The family of parrotfish is one of the most common fish families found in the Galapagos and many individual species within this family inhabit the archipelago.

BOTTLENOSE DOLPHIN

It is the most common and well-known dolphin. Can be seen riding the bow wave in front of boats. The life span of dolphins in Galapagos is around 25 years but some bottlenose dolphins may live up to 50 years old.

MARINE IGUANA

It is an iguana found only on the Galapagos Islands that has the ability, unique among modern lizards, to live and forage in the sea, making it a marine reptile.

GALAPAGOS GIANT TORTOISE

It is the largest living species of tortoise, reaching weights of over 400 kg (880 lb). With life spans in the wild of over 100 years, it is one of the longest-lived vertebrates. A captive individual lived at least 170 years. Shell size and shape vary between populations.

ALBATROSS GALAPAGOS BIRD

It is endemic to this archipelago. The Albatross bird is the largest bird in the Galapagos Islands. They are extremely loyal birds to each other whereby when a male finds a female mating partner, they will stay together and raise their chicks until one of them dies.

HAMMERHEAD SHARK

This shark can be seen almost in every island of the Galapagos Archipelago. Most of the hammerheads are very social animals. Their oddly-shaped heads make them very recognizable.

RED FOOTED BOOBY

This is the smallest of the three Galapagos species of boobies and tends to perch and nest in trees rather than being ground based like the others.

GALAPAGOS SEA LION

This is one of the most numerous species in the Galapagos Archipelago. They prefer sandy beaches and gentle rocky shores. Their loud "bark", playful nature, and graceful agility in water make them the "welcoming party" of the islands.

GALAPAGOS SHORT EARED OWL

The Galapagos owls prey on birds, rats and lizards. They are found on many of the Galapagos Islands. Sometimes these owls fly between islands looking for food.

GALAPAGOS FRIGATEBIRD

Frigatebird reproduction is one of those amazing examples of animal behavior to observe in Galapagos Islands. Males start off everything with a very basic flat surface, while hormonal changes will produce color changes, like the impressive scarlet red gular pouch. The pouch becomes fully inflated

GALAPAGOS FINCHES

Their beaks and shapes reflect their specializations. Finches' birds are all brownish or black but have different song melodies.

FLAMINGO

They are very shy birds, unlike much wildlife in Galapagos. Their food (specially the crustaceans) is full of substances called carotenoid pigments that cause flamingos' feathers to become pink.

SALLY LIGHTFOOD CRAB

It is one of the many charismatic species that inhabit the Galapagos Islands, and is often seen sharing the seaside rocks with the marine iguanas.

GALAPAGOS GREEN TURTLE

It is found hugely and continuously in Galapagos. The Galapagos Islands provide the main nesting areas for green sea turtles, this is why the nesting colony of Galapagos is one of the largest in the East Pacific Ocean.

BLUE FOOTED BOOBY

These are among the most famous birds in the Galapagos Islands, because it is the most commonly seen booby bird in this archipelago as it nests near the coast in many of the islands and also feeds close to shore.

CHARLES DARWIN (1809 - 1882)

The most celebrated visitor to Galapagos was the young Charles Darwin in 1835 on board H.M.S. Beagle. His five-year voyage on Beagle has become legendary, as insights gained by the bright young scientist on his trip to exotic places greatly influenced his masterwork, the book On the Origin of Species.

After considerable explorations in South America, the Beagle reached the Galapagos Islands. In there, Darwin found a remarkable population of plants, birds and reptiles that had developed in isolation from the mainland, but often differed on almost identical islands next door to one another, and whose characteristics he could only explain by a gradual transformation of the various species.

DARWIN FINCHES

Also known as the Galapagos finches, are a group of 14 species of birds. They were first collected by Charles Darwin on the Galapagos Islands during the second voyage of the Beagle. Thirteen are found on the Galapagos Islands and one on Cocos Island. These finches probably descended from one type of ancestor and then, due to isolation and through chance, different climates and natural forces such as food availability and type, they evolved into thirteen different types of finches in the Galapagos.

The most important differences between these species are in the size and shape of their beaks, that are highly adapted to different food sources. Recent studies in Galapagos on the beaks of the finches have provided striking new evidence on the operation of natural selection in real time.

Large cactus finch

Large ground finch

Medium ground finch

Cactus finch

Sharp-beaked ground finch

Small ground finch

Woodpecker finch

Vegetarian tree finch

Medium tree finch

Large tree finch

Small tree finch

Warbler finch

Mangrove finch